T0065719

BOOKS BY

REYNOLDS PRICE

REYNOLDS PRICE

LETTER TO A MAN IN THE FIRE

DOES GOD EXIST AND DOES HE CARE?

A TOUCHSTONE BOOK

PUBLISHED BY SIMON & SCHUSTER

NEW YORK LONDON TORONTO SYDNEY SINGAPORE

TOUCHSTONE
Rockefeller Center
1230 Avenue of the Americas
New York, NY 10020

Set in Electra

Manufactured in the United States of America

1   3   5   7   9   10   8   6   4   2

The Library of Congress has cataloged the Scribner edition
as follows:
Price, Reynolds, 1933–
Letter to a man in the fire :
does God exist and does he care? / Reynolds Price.
p.   cm.
1. God. 2. Fox, Jim, 1962–1998. I. Title.
BT102.P725   1999
231 — dc21   98-54197
CIP

ISBN 0-684-85627-1
ISBN 978-0-684-85627-8

LETTER TO A MAN IN THE FIRE

FOR

JIM FOX

1962–1998

PREFACE

One especially fine afternoon in April 1997, I received two letters, both unexpected and each with contents that complicated the pleasures of the day. The first I opened was from Auburn Theological Seminary in New York City. It invited me to give the Jack and Lewis Rudin Lecture at the Seminary sometime in the coming autumn. Their only specification was a lecture on a freely chosen subject of interest to the students of such an institution. Lately, obliged to concentrate, I've declined opportunities to speak in churches or other religious institutions of whatever creed; so I folded the letter from Auburn and thought I'd surely decline it.

The second letter of that afternoon, however, was as compelling a communication as I've ever got. It was a blunt inquiry from a young man named Jim Fox—a stranger to me—who'd recently been forced to withdraw from medical school because of the recurrence in his body of an avid cancer. He had read a book of mine, A *Whole New Life*, published in 1994. It's a book that recounts my ordeal in the 1980s with spinal cancer. The young man's letter was of such a brief and un-self-pitying eloquence that—despite my inadequacy in the face of its enormous questions about the existence of God and the nature of God's care, if any, for his creatures—I knew I had no choice but to answer it.

Haste was plainly called for, so I responded quickly and no doubt helplessly in a single telephone contact. That helplessness left me feeling, before the week passed, that I should take the opportunity of the Rudin lecture at Auburn and make myself face the young man's questions more thoughtfully and at greater length. I'd write the lecture as a longer reply to my young correspondent. I accepted Auburn's offer then, began to read and think; and I continued sporadic correspondence by e-mail with the young man through the summer as his health seemed to worsen. We were hundreds of miles apart, had never met; and our brief exchanges were unconcerned with his first big questions. But I hoped that these simple exchanges might say the better part of what I meant on the matters that troubled him.

In the summer he sent me the manuscripts of a few short stories he'd written. They expressed a watchful eye and a patent intelligence, but I was unable to think they were publishable. I suggested instead, and honestly, that I suspected his fruitful subject would be his ordeal. There is still a very slender body of readable witness from the endurers and survivors of the kind of scalding he knew so intimately. His next note seemed to take my suggestion in good spirit. All the while, I was reading and making notes for the letter I intended for him and for Auburn. Unsure that I'd have even the scaffolding of an interesting response, I delayed telling him of my plan or its progress.

In the early fall, he wrote to say that he'd decided against returning to medical school for the coming term. A new form of treatment was proving hard. That news hastened me forward in my plan. It seemed better that he see my letter than that Auburn get its lecture. Midway through the fall, then, when I'd finished what felt like a presentable draft — and before I risked intruding on a man in more trouble than I knew — I wrote to my correspondent. No answer. Soon I tried phoning again, in the attempt to invite him to New York for the lecture and the dinner that would follow. At the very least, I hoped to send him my manuscript; but though his pleasant taped voice still spoke on his answering machine, he made no contact in return.

Since his home was far off, and I knew no one among his family and friends, I saw no other immediate choice; and on November 3rd 1997, I read that initial draft of my letter at Auburn Seminary to a courteous audience of students, faculty, and guests. In a brief introduction, I told the audience of my correspondent's April letter; and when I'd completed the reading, I replied to a question about his present condition by saying that I honestly feared he was dead. Once home, I phoned again. No reply beyond his taped calm voice.

Saddened that a stranger—who for months had been so near the midst of my thoughts that he'd come to seem a friend—should have vanished, I resolved to return to work at once, expanding and clarifying the letter in the hope that, failing to reach its original aim, the text might find some use in the hands of others. Additions have more than doubled the length of the draft I read at Auburn. It's longer now than anything I'd have risked volunteering to send to a gravely ill person. But its shape, its tenor, and its steady concern for two large questions remain unchanged. Its title is the merest acknowledgment of my friend's hope and the failure that I must have added to so many others he experienced.

As I was at work on this final draft, I felt the compulsion to know his news at least—this unseen man who'd caught my attention. Yet there was, after all, the chance of the slow but extraordinary kind of recovery that I and some others had experienced. If that had occurred, then all I'd written should at least have the light of his rescue raked backward across it. So I made another call in early December and again reached his tape.

Baffled and beginning to wonder if his family had somehow kept the recorded voice intact after his death, I left another request that he phone me. By then I was allowing for the possibility that, whatever his health, he might have regretted the request he'd made and no longer wished to talk with me. Unknowingly, I might have failed some expectation he'd had in making first contact eight months earlier.

But that night I received a call from a friend of his, a woman who said that he'd asked her to phone me. Through her, he sent me greetings but told me of his reluctance to talk. His friend spoke of a rapid decline and deep depression and said that she could not imagine his "making it far into the new year." He had told me, in our only phone conversation, that he'd entered medical school after several years on Wall Street, but I hadn't wanted to ask his age.

I was familiar, from my own dark time, with such a reticence in lives under active assault. It often flows from a shutting down on all other concerns and distractions except the still hard glint of survival. The focus on that glint can blank all else and can often prove crucial in the hope to last. That radical clear aim can also become a serene death watch. In the face of such news then, I felt that to send the letter so late might border on cruelty. I knew that few of its ideas would seem new to a well-read adult, but a number of my questions and suggestions are hardly conventional consolation. So I sent him my best hopes through the woman. Then I wrote him briefly of the service he'd done me with his questions, and I mentioned having read the letter at Auburn.

If he'd had the strength, the need, or the patience to read it, I'd have sent it on; but I heard nothing more till Jim's friend phoned again on February 24th '98 to tell me of his death the previous day. She'd been right. He hadn't made it far into the new year, and he'd died at the age of thirty-five. She said that— except for a few last unconscious days—he died as himself, closely tended by his family and in his own home.

No other response can stand for the one I didn't receive. In one large sense, I'm left in the baffling silence of one hand beating the empty air—my lone hand oaring in the wake of a friend's departure. I'm unlikely, soon if ever, to know his estimate of the sanity or the wasteful folly of the time I've spent or the

words I've ventured (the recommendations for further reading, listening, and looking were added after
Jim's death). But I'm surely grateful for his willingness
to reach out on the near-edge of a stark abyss and
honor me with his questions — the largest of all. Subsequent thanks go to the faculty and staff of Auburn
Seminary for their welcome in November 1997, to
Jack and Lewis Rudin for their generosity in estab-
lishing the ongoing lecture series, and to Carolyn
Reidy, Susan Moldow, Nan Graham, Frank Lentric-
chia, David Aers, Daniel Voll, Eric Larson, and Har-
riet Wasserman, who made helpful suggestions and
encouraged its publication. After my correspondent's
death, his sister Mary contacted me generously. She
has since told me much of her brother's vivid life; and
she's given me a picture of him, taken only eight
months before his death. The face is almost startling
in the boldness with which his Celtic blue eyes and
bold jaw confront the world still with a watchful readi-
ness, no trace of fear.

R.P.

LETTER TO A MAN
IN THE FIRE

Dear Jim,

It hardly seems appropriate to thank you for letting me know the hard facts of the cancer which has interrupted your medical training. A malignancy in the colon with a spread to the liver and pancreas sounds more daunting to me than the threat of my own tumor years ago. Mine was confined to the spinal cord. As you know, it managed to paralyze both my legs; but with heroic care from others, its threat was turned and has been absent for long years now. Still, hard as your news is, I feel some thanks that the even harder questions you ask have pressed on me a need to think my way again, if only in the most personal manner, into the bottomless mystery of suffering.

I understand that you've contacted me because you know, from my own cancer memoir, that I've survived, though with paralyzed legs from the tumor that gave every sign of killing me when it was discovered in 1984. And you know as well how strongly I believe—from several kinds of evidence—that the means of my survival worked outward from a sense of God's awareness of my ordeal and his willingness to watch and to brace me, generally in deep silence, in my own fierce hope to live.

Beyond that one credential—and a lifetime of watching the world fairly closely and reading widely, and the fact that you've contacted me—you must know from the start that I have no further potent claim to make on your time or credulity. I'm no trained theologian, no regular churchgoer, no mathematical cosmologist, no theoretical physicist, and no statistician with an eye for your chances or anyone else's. What I do claim to be is a watchful human in his seventh decade who harbored a similar killing invader deep in his body a few years ago and who thinks he was saved by a caring, though enigmatic, God.

In the face of those limits, you've asked me two ancient and sizable questions which, given the facts of your present trials, I'll attempt to look at, however partially. You know that they're questions I've stared in the teeth on more than one occasion since the agonized death of my father from lung cancer when I was twenty-one and he was a young fifty-four years old, with nearly four decades of smoking behind him. While you don't state your bafflements outright, it seems to me that you've implied your questions in these sentences from your letter—

I want to believe in a God who cares . . . because I may meet him sooner than I had expected. I think I am at the point where I can accept the existence of a God (otherwise I can't explain the origin of the universe), but I can't yet believe he cares about us.

What I hear you asking, in the slimmest summary, is this—

1. Was our universe created by an intelligent power; and if so, is the Creator conscious of its creatures and benignly concerned for their lives?
2. If the answer to both halves of that question is Yes, how can a gifted young human being be tormented and perhaps killed early?

I've already asserted a troubled Yes to the first of your mysteries. And the Yes is firm enough in its groundings to make me wonder how any close observer can believe otherwise. What's *troubled* in the Yes is my inability to prove the truth of my claim to others. Nonetheless, what I assert with no serious doubt is that our one universe anyhow was created and is maintained by a single divine intelligence who still exists and continues to oversee his primeval handiwork. I'll refer to that God, as the Jewish-Christian-Islamic tradition does, with masculine pronouns; and I hew to that tradition, with all the problems it brings, not in male pride but because I suspect that there's more than a chance that God's revelation of his nature as *male* could offer a chink of light on the question of who God is.

Beyond that assertion of private faith, I can offer no other person any evidence more convincing than the patterns that I think I've detected in my own history, in certain private intensities which I'll describe, and in the final fact that — repeating the words of an old philosophy professor of mine — "A belief in God, and in the immortality of the soul, has tended to be the opinion of a vast majority of the human race." His claim has always seemed reasonable to me, and the majority opinion of Homo sapiens throughout our known history is worth, at a minimum, initial respect. Yet I'm more than aware that such an assertion of belief from me, or any other human being in whatever time or place, may be of no more value than a paranoid's conviction that the CIA has planted a listening device in his molars.

My belief in a Creator derives largely from detailed and overpowering personal intuition, an unshakable hunch, and a set of demonstrations that go far back in my consciousness—well before I began to comprehend the details of the world of deeply held but unoppressive Christian faith in which my parents had been formed, and in which they raised me. What I've called *demonstrations* have come in a very few experiences of my own, beginning when I was six years old.

Starting on a warm afternoon in the summer of 1939, when I was wandering alone in the pine woods by our suburban house in piedmont North Carolina, I've experienced moments of sustained calm awareness that subsequent questioning has never discounted. Those moments, which recurred at unpredictable and widely spaced intervals till some thirteen years ago, still seem to me undeniable manifestations of the Creator's benign, or patiently watchful, interest in particular stretches of my life, though perhaps not all of it. And each of the moments—never lasting for more than seconds but seeming, in retrospect, hours long—has taken the form of sudden and entirely unsought breakings-in upon my consciousness of a demonstration that all of visible and invisible nature (myself included) is a single reality, a single thought from a central mind.

To be more descriptive, in those moments or openings—which are far from exotic in humankind (Wordsworth's accounts, in *The Prelude* and other poems, of similar findings in his youth are the classic description, as I learned years after my own began)— I've heard what amounts to a densely complex yet piercingly direct harmony that appears to come from the heart of whatever reality made us and watches our lives.

There've been no shows of light, no gleaming illusory messengers, almost no words; and the music that underlies each moment is silent but felt in every cell like a grander pulse beneath my own. Always simultaneously, I've been assured that this reality is launched on a history that's immensely longer than any life span I can hope to have and that it's designed to end in some form of transformation and eternal entry into the presence of that central mind, God.

If I were not nervous, in the prescribed modern fashion, I'd call such experiences revelations. I'll repeat that they've come exceedingly rarely, no more than four times in my entire life; and only twice have they taken a visual or audible form—the moment when Jesus washed my cancer wound and the moment, weeks later, when my legs were plainly failing. Alone in a dark bed, I asked how much more pain I must suffer; and a voice answered *More*.

Still, the experiences were as real as any car wreck. They've proved overwhelming in their unanswerability, and their power has meant that I've literally never had to make the touted "leap of faith" into sudden belief. Belief came toward me early, as it's come to many others. To say so is no boast. Many men, women, and children have been far more richly gifted than I with such grace; and it's worth remarking that belief confers no necessary bliss on its recipient. When I was a college student, I asked Elizabeth Bowen, the novelist, about the religion of her friend T. S. Eliot; and my question implied that his adult embrace of Anglo-Catholicism had been a retreat. Bowen took the question seriously but then said that belief was often a more difficult course than many others.

Till now, I don't claim unusual difficulties. The usual lions have appeared in the road, the usual boulders crash on through the roof, I go on lapsing into old and new faults. But since those childhood openings, there's been no sustained time in my life when—in the aftermath of all absurdities and disasters—I couldn't repeat what Tertullian said, in effect, in the second century—*Credo quia absurdum est*, "I believe *because* it's absurd." And that affirmation is made, not in the blind embrace of an empty irrational hope of love-from-the-sky but in full possession of what I take to be ample proof.

The scarcity of what I've called personal openings is one of the reasons I've taken them seriously. If they'd come with any frequency, I'd suspect myself of brain damage or unconscious fraud—or a sanctity that is patently unavailable to me. But I'm further persuaded by the fact that my occasional references in memoirs to such private moments have elicited dozens of letters from apparently lucid strangers who attest to similar experiences and who then confide that I'm the first person to whom they've mentioned their curious luck. I've come to suspect that, far from being the exclusive experience of saints and mystics, many more perfectly normal human beings than we can easily imagine share such dawnings and keep them secret in some desire to avoid the appearance of lunacy.

A remarkable writer, who's eighty-seven years old, has recently confirmed my suspicion and sent me this description of one such opening she herself has experienced—

> . . . such inner events are much more common than people dare to admit. They carry their own authentication, I think, in the atmosphere of complete simplicity and great depth that surrounds them. Mine came, like yours, at a time of medical stress, during some exhausting tests

before an operation. I can't exactly say "it came"
though; it was rather that I went out to meet
it. . . . This time I went out along the Galilee hills
and came to a crowd gathered around a man,
and I stood on the outskirts intending to listen.
But he looked over the crowd at me and then
said, "What do you want?" I said, "Could you
send someone to come with me and help me
stand up after the tests, because I can't manage
alone?" He thought for a minute and then said,
"How would it be if I came?"

Few events I've heard of elsewhere are as plain or as
convincing as that. The very words in which my correspondent describes her encounter have a clarity
and a last-moment grasp which rivals, in contemporary diction, that ultimate dawn meeting of the fish-
ing disciples with their risen Lord at the end of the
Gospel of John. From the shore he directs their boat
and their net toward a big school of fish; but when
they land the catch, they discover that he has already
roasted a breakfast of fish and bread.

Impressive as my own openings were, and remain
for me, their witness to a still-existing Creator was
supported powerfully and far more steadily by my
early luck in having haplessly generous parents, kind
and guileless as the best of children, who guided my

early intimations into a quiet variety of sane attention to ultimate concerns. So from childhood till now that attentive worship has largely been private, not institutional, and has mostly been grounded in the figure of Jesus, son of God and man.

My worship has also been informed and braced by my reading, primarily in Hebrew and Christian scriptures and in ancient and modern theology. I'll try to make clear, as I proceed, that most of those theologians were either physicists or artists—novelists, poets, painters, composers. Only occasionally have I studied professional thinkers about the mysteries of life, having seldom found one who spoke to my own concerns. A lifetime's friendships, enmities, loves, and solitudes, and four decades of teaching have also contributed their weight; and the effort to bring the heft of those findings into daily life and work has been continuous, though often more than regrettably sporadic.

Even more powerfully, I've been supported by the manifest conviction of the world's supreme artists—the classic Buddhist and Hindu scriptures, sculptures, and sacred music; the cathedrals of medieval Europe; and the painting, poetry, and music of burdened but staunch believers such as Dante, Michelangelo, Donne, Milton, Bach, Handel, and W. H. Auden. (Though Auden is a far more recent name to place in such august company—he died in 1973—I'm convinced that his voluminous poetry and critical prose have earned him a place in such surroundings. I had the luck to know him and study with him in graduate school in England in the mid-1950s. There—in his late forties, before age and physical decay marooned him in a painful solitude—his outrageous but always humane intelligence and wit were powerful carriers of his unblinking scrutiny of God and the world and the brilliance and shy warmth of his best poems, secular or sacred, are still firm guarantors of his findings and claims.)

I don't know of the occurrence in your life of any such events or meetings, so I have no sense of whether you've had external hints of the existence and attention of a transcendent reality. I've known many men and women who claim to have had none, even in troubled straits. And since I've claimed that my own early acceptance of the fact of God derives from such events, you'd be more than fair to ask what I might say to anyone who's experienced no such clues—or has got negative intimations of meaninglessness or even malice at the heart of things.

In the absence of some such confirmation of meaning, what can a still-searching man or woman do? I'm aware of how empty, even demented, my claim may sound, especially to anyone in present and unrelieved trouble. But since you've asked me your questions, my single assertion—and the body of my life's written work—is the substance of what I have to offer. If you go on to ask what a searcher may do to make an earnest start—especially a searcher as well-informed as you— I'm afraid I could offer little more than a proposal which you may feel you've already exhausted: the shamefaced suggestion that you go on waiting as long as you can at the one main door, requesting entry from whatever power may lie beyond it.

Prayer is not a language in which I'm proficient. I've read the prayers of saints and martyrs, the reflections on prayer of Teresa of Avila, John of the Cross, and their very few peers; and I've admired their powers of invention and stillness. But my own prayers, though frequent in hard times, have mostly been either repetitions of ancient models (the Lord's Prayer, the Apostles' Creed, the Jesus prayer, the Hail Mary) or brief private requests, generated in word and aim by the weight of a given moment in my present life or the lives of those near me.

And it's been my finding, and the finding of many famous doubters, that the simplest prayer reiterated in the face of silence—*Stand by me here* or *Guide me on* or *Face this creature you've brought to life and show him that this is at least your will*—may slowly or suddenly pry a chink of reliable light, a half-open window, a

glimpse of a maybe passable road. Sudden floods of
assurance have come, unsought, to certain reluctant
men and women — Paul of Tarsus, for instance, or the
Emperor Constantine or Simone Weil at that crucial
moment in 1938 when she felt that Christ was present
in her room: "A presence more personal, more certain,
and more real than that of a human being." Both the
silent and the seismic responses to such assurance
have been enacted numerous times in our history. But
it's well to note, at every point, that there's no guarantee that any prayer — modest or grand — will receive a
remotely detectable answer but you surely know that.

Behind my own convictions, of course — and
implicit in my claim to have had personal demonstrations of God's existence when many of my friends
have had none — lie private questions, one of which
is common. I come from a part of America — the site
of the blood-and-guilt-drenched old slave-owning
Confederacy — in which Calvinist notions arrive in
our mother's milk, notions of our helpless election by
God to an eternal salvation or damnation. That
dreadful conclusion of John Calvin's seems confirmed by a good deal that's happened in my particular world and by much that I've undergone and
witnessed in my own mind and body, so I'm compelled to say that I'm profoundly uncertain of
whether or not the Creator notices and *loves* every

creature as much as another. I mean *love* in all its best human senses, unable to fathom God's own definition.

And no one who's had my early brushes with the devastating logic of Calvin's doctrine of predestination could deny that even Jesus' assurance that the very hairs of our heads are numbered can be taken to mean that God *knows* the detailed sum of our qualities and actions without necessarily approving us or loving us. It's worth noticing also that Jesus' assertions about God are made to particular historical audiences—the Jews and Gentiles of first-century Palestine who chose to stop and hear him. His teaching may not always have been intended for the remainder of humankind, in all ages.

It has seemed to me for years that there may well be many human beings of whom the Creator takes sporadic notice, if any. Few believers known to me have survived to midlife without the sense of occasional, or frequent, desertions by God or absences of his interest or—hardest of all—his intentional silences. It was no accident that I felt compelled as a relatively buoyant undergraduate to write a long paper on the influence of Saint John of the Cross's descriptions of the Dark Night of the Soul on the poetry of T. S. Eliot. (Eliot, that most affluent and meticulously dressed of all the half-blind trekkers through the wastes of God's deser-

tion, was very much alive as I wrote. Far the most hon-
ored English poet since Tennyson, he looked still, in
photographs from the 1950s, like a nearly starved heron
miles short of an oasis.)

Even the most generous-hearted saints have
reported such parched treks through the silent deserts
of melancholia, disease, and the hatred of their ene-
mies; and even at the age of twenty, I sensed that danger for me if I went on living as my sense of a writer's
life appeared to demand—a long silent watch on the
world, then decades of solitary reporting. A single
bleak statistic speaks to such absences of hope and foresight; some twenty percent of Americans who seek
medical help with clinical depression will eventually
kill themselves in despair. And a psychiatrist, who is
herself a bipolar manic-depressive, claimed recently
on CNN that, early in the new century, such self-
violence will be the second leading cause of adult
death in the United States.

I should add quickly, though, that I have no sense
whatever that God chooses to notice individuals who
look especially "noticeable" by our standards of personal worth or social standing. The stinking wretch
on the frozen pavement, the abandoned orphan in a
Romanian warehouse of unwanted children, may be
of more concern to God than I and all my social
peers. Certainly the steady notice of God is likely to

cause eventual suffering, as the lives of virtually all saints show. Think only of Joan of Arc chained to the stake but alive in the flames, crying "Jesus, Jesus"; of Francis of Assisi pierced through hands and feet with the bleeding wounds of his Lord; of Bernadette of Lourdes consumed by her own hungry tumor that ate her, young, with no trace of mercy.

Of course if we assume with Calvin that some human lives are chosen by the Creator, from all eternity, to be damned and destroyed, then God—or God the Father—must be seen as a menacing force, a force so far past the comprehension of even the most fervent mystic or the bravest theologian as to make our secular contemplation all but pointless. And with that same presumption of Calvin's (and before him, of the even more formidable Augustine), it would seem that the choices which predestine our behavior and our final destination have been made, for unrecoverable reasons that at least hint of conscious cruelty on God's part, far beyond the realms of human comprehension.

Thus any questions that an individual may ultimately ask about the meaning of his or her destiny will be idle gaming in a very long night—long by the infinitesimal standards of humankind. And while I can see that such a predisposing God is deducible from certain speeches in Hebrew scripture, certain words of Jesus,

from outright claims in Paul's epistles (most vividly in
his letter to the Ephesians, which may not be by Paul
but has always had canonical standing in Christian
scripture), and from the occasional real-life spectacle
of a man or woman who seems undeniably cursed, I
nonetheless recall quite plainly the many instants
through multiple years in which I've soberly contem-
plated acts or words I knew to be dead-wrong or -right
and have then deliberately chosen wrong or right in
crystal clarity of will and aim.

So my inveterate conviction of personal freedom
compels me — as it does most men and women, I suspect — to reject any hidebound belief in pre-election
and predestination. Some of our choices seem to
flow spontaneously from the facts and needs of a
given moment; other choices feel inevitable, even
fated; and we appear to have imperfect control over
that difference. I feel convinced, however, that no
one soul is damned from the start by a dice-throwing
God. It seems more likely to me that all are, in some
inscrutable way, saved forever. To indicate that such
statements are no mere personal whim, I could go
on, for instance, to point out also how drastically an
outright Saved or Damned notion of Fate—a faith
that even no Greek dramatist quite claims—collides
with those assurances from Jesus and occasional earlier prophets that we are the children of a loving and

merciful parental God (though I'll glance later at other speeches in which Jesus portrays an angry avenging final Judge).

Nonetheless, I'm prepared to ask if one of the most damaging weaknesses of modern Christianity and of some branches of Judaism doesn't arise as a direct result of our passionate need to believe both in our individual freedom and our innate worth—our deep-rooted conviction that we deserve and have amply earned the particular close attention of God. That resulting weakness is most visible in the insistence by centuries of clergy and generations of hungry souls that God, the Maker and Keeper of billions of galaxies of stars and planets seething in their violence, is literally our personal father as well—and a father, we're told, who is even more attentive and caring than the best of earthly fathers.

We're constantly asked to trust in the soothing voices which tell us that the stoker of the furnace of the most immense suns, the delicate fashioner (through the instrument of evolution) of the hummingbird's wings, the infant's lungs, the white shark's jaws, and the AIDS virus is likewise the architect and builder of one's own fragile body—the very fingers with which I write these blundering words. And not only is he my Maker and yours, he is steadily attuned to our needs and fears and has the final purpose of bringing us toward him in a union of everlasting bliss. Or so we're taught in the churches and some of the synagogues known to me and in most of the enduring prose and poetry of the Christian tradition.

To be sure, in one astonishingly intimate and apparently unique moment, Jesus addresses God as *abba*, the Aramaic informal word for *father*. It is one of the rare moments when we can be sure that we are hearing what scholars call the *ipsissima verba* of Jesus, the convincing word and voice in which he spoke on a given occasion (as we are similarly convinced when he often introduces, rather than concludes, his most solemn remarks with the words *Amen amen*, Hebrew words which the King James version translates as *Verily, verily*). Surely any father whom the adult Jesus can address as *abba* will hear all his prayers and answer them with good — with bread not stones, fish not serpents.

Elsewhere in the Gospels, Jesus extends that promise to all his hearers and perhaps to the remainder of humanity — God may be every human's benign father. Despite the distinguished credentials which such promises bear, however, they've always been as doubtful as they are welcome among realistically wary believers. No theological learning is required, after all, to stand in the ashes of one's private hopes or beside the literal ashes of an innocent loved one — a five-year-old son, say, who has died before our eyes in the torment of leukemia—and to wonder, from that point in human time and place, just where *abba* is now to be found. What precisely is *abba*'s address at the scalding moment? What line will now reach him and will he reply? In an unbroken note of the most serious eloquence, from the known beginnings of sacred poetry, the cry of humankind has begged to know how the hand that made us has likewise struck us down or has let some other force destroy us.

I can only glance here at the Christian mystery of the Trinity—a belief in the existence of one God consisting of three persons: Father, Son, and Holy Spirit. I attempt to lighten that crucial obscurity for the students in my class in Milton's poetry by suggesting to them that, young as they are, they already comprise several distinct yet united persons—they may be, for instance, simultaneously and completely Child, Lover, Student, Mother, or Father. (Milton's private views on the Trinity were mildly heretical, though the fact is all but invisible in *Paradise Lost*.)

Belief in the Trinity is of such a dangerous complexity that many contemporary believers have ironed it out to their own comfort, a comfort that comes close to faith in several gods. Many Christians are unaware of a grievous misunderstanding when they attempt to see the Son of God and the Holy Spirit as our sources of boundless mercy while the Father becomes the distant and eventually negligible principle of law and justice. But Christian scripture and a close attention to human experience provide little defense for a dodge that tries to imagine the Father's punishing you through your child's illness while the Son and the Holy Spirit attend to the child's healing—or its safe transport to Heaven, if the Father's anger rejects all prayers.

At this hard point, again I hear your final question — does God care about us? It's surely a question that, in the Genesis story of the first generation of humans, is only the third puzzlement to arise in the minds of our mythical ancestors. We can safely assume that Adam, waking in Eden for the first time, will promptly ask what Milton's new Adam asks in *Paradise Lost*, book eight—

> . . . how came I thus, how here?
> Not of my self; by some great Maker then,
> In goodness and in power pre-eminent;
> Tell me, how may I know him, how adore,
> From whom I have that thus I move and live,
> And feel that I am happier than I know.

The second human question would appear then to be Adam's "Why am I alone?"—a curiosity which occasions the gift of Eve, God's bringing her to birth from Adam's side. And Eve's first, though unstated, question may well be why Adam at once assumes dominance over her, a mystery to which she's given no direct answer in Hebrew or Christian scripture. But Adam's third question is directed again to God after Adam has joined Eve in eating the single forbidden fruit, and it comes with more than a hint of self-pity—"Why was I created insufficient to observe God's single command of obedience?" or "Why make a world in which your creatures are doomed to pain and death?" (Eve, with sober dignity in both Genesis and Milton, accepts her share of blame in the first calamitous disobedience; and she declines to claim personal insufficiency, saying only "The serpent beguiled me and I ate.")

Whoever first asked that third question, it has ever since been stated flatly by our species as "Why does evil occur in the domain of a God who claims benign concern for his creatures?" And by *evil*, virtually all of us mean what Eve must have meant when she first saw her son Abel's body, killed by his brother Cain. Evil, we believe, is a condition arising unpredictably in our daily lives and productive of suffering—often to the point of death—in individuals as small as an infant and in groups as huge as an entire people. Examples of that range of agony have crowded around us with special frequency in the past century (or is that apparent frequency only the result of our being so incessantly informed by television and the press?).

It's important, anyhow, to emphasize that the individual human's recognition of the arrival of evil is preceded by an actual experience of extreme pain—physical, psychic, or both. The descent of evil upon a whole group—American Indians, the Jews of Europe, Cambodians, the Tutsis, the homeless pariahs of every country—may be initially harder to measure but are even more baffling, especially for those of us reared in a nation and an age that assured us of God's unbounded benevolence.

My own religious education developed in a Christian family consisting of a Methodist mother, a Baptist father, and aunts and uncles who were divided among the Episcopal, Methodist, and Presbyterian churches. Again, none of my near relations was steadily devout nor hotly sectarian nor was any one of them involved in an apparent concern for theological brooding, though they enjoyed an occasional Sunday afternoon's front-porch volley on, say, the superiority of total-immersion baptism over the few sprinkled drops of a christening.

My Baptist father, for one, took keen delight in pointing out that his Methodist in-laws were demonstrably *not* baptized since they'd undergone a mere sprinkling in childhood whereas Jesus had been totally immersed in the River Jordan (otherwise how could the Gospel of Matthew say that, once dipped, Jesus "came up from the water"?). And my father's maiden aunt Belle relished reminding her Episcopalian nieces that their church was founded by Henry VIII while her own Baptist church was of course founded by Jesus and named for his cousin John. But such more-than-half-serious banter seemed never to diminish my kin's unquestioned faith in God's attention to their every move.

The sufferings of individual members of our families were both severe and quite normal for the time and place — the post-Reconstruction, mid-Depression South. There was a great deal of untreated clinical depression among the women, to the point of one attempted and one successful suicide; and there was sustained and widely punitive alcoholism among the men, one of whom also killed himself. It's occurred to me in recent years that the men may well have been self-medicating their own depression, a choice which was simply unavailable to the women of their time and place. That, I think, was my own father's story, though he managed at last to walk away from drinking by the age of thirty-six — no help from Alcoholics Anonymous or from any other therapist but his Baptist minister and my mother's love.

Yet, whatever the trouble, all my kin appeared to accept the explanation that their pain was likely to be the result of some incalculable and inconsistent response by God to wrongdoing in the adults among us. Our elders seemed confident that they suffered for their own sins and the sins of their forebears. Their young children suffered both for their parents' sins and, mysteriously as we all did, from the unfathomable but unchallengeable will of God.

Only one pair of us—my mother's youngest brother and his wife—experienced an agony that could not be charged to their own failings. Their only child, a beautiful daughter and my first cousin, died at age nine in the howling torture of a massive bone infection. In later years my mother would often tell me how, in her niece's death throes, "Little Frances's body would twist itself back into nearly a hoop with the terrible pain, and her lips were as crisp and dry as burned paper."

But though my kin were frankly aware of their own failings and those of their relations, the conviction that *individual* sin was a cause for such mysterious suffering didn't seem strong among us. There was very little guilty breast-beating or finger-pointing blame. Our sense of sin was more generic, more nearly our foregone lot as human creatures than it was any one man's or woman's earned curse. And I'll confess that a sense of personal guilt has never been a strong thread in whatever fabric I've managed to weave overhead for my own understanding and protection.

I noted in my early reading of the Gospels that Jesus appears to contradict himself on the subject of personal responsibility for suffering. There are the famous speeches in which he predicts a coming judgment on the wicked; and no such moment is more impressive than the one with which Jesus concludes the Sermon on the Mount in Matthew 7—

> "Not everyone who says to me, 'Lord, Lord,' will enter the kingdom of heaven, but only the one who does the will of my Father in heaven. On that day many will say to me, 'Lord, Lord, did we not prophesy in your name, and cast out demons in your name, and do many deeds of power in your name?' Then I will declare to them, 'I never knew you; go away from me, you evildoers.' "

Yet in Luke 13, Jesus asserts the innocence of one particular group of killed men. Then he turns to his audience and threateningly demands their own hurried repentance. In a contradiction which has caused oceans of subsequent pain, he says

> ". . . those eighteen who were killed when the tower of Siloam fell on them—do you think that

they were worse offenders than all the others living in Jerusalem? No, I tell you; but unless you
repent, you will all perish just as they did."

I have no reluctance in believing that a just God
who chooses to survey the human spectacle will find
sources of outrage so flagrant as to warrant his respond-
ing with a ferocity that may consume bystanders who
are more or less innocent. Equally, from the short
perspective of human time, he can seem to ignore
gigantic wrongs. Yet our ever-increasing knowledge
of the unthinkably vast scale of the universe does
not impinge upon my ability to believe that a just
God may sustain his evidently sporadic interest in the
moral choices of a species as minuscule as our own.

The example of computers alone, new and primi-
tive as they still are, is sufficient to demonstrate that a
single intelligence (even an artificial one) may
steadily monitor many million shifting bits of infor-
mation. And the abundance of a single human failing—adult cruelty to children, which we've only
begun to contemplate with any degree of honesty—
is enough, in my eyes, to trigger a vengeful gesture
from God, however distant.

But I feel no impulse, and certainly no right, to
ask him to attend to my own desires for vengeance,
for instance, or to ask you to consider what wrongs of

your own might have triggered your present illness. My strong inclination is to deny that God keeps such accounts, though I do anticipate some settling of the balances for maybe all creatures in whatever form our last judgment takes. (Most religions anticipate some such reckoning, however harsh or mild.)

You know from my memoir that in the first weeks of my return from radical surgery and ensuing depression, I experienced what I can only call a vision. It came on a morning just before my five weeks of scalding radiation began, and it took the shape of an utterly real dawn encounter with Jesus on the shore of the Lake of Galilee and then waist-deep in its water. As his disciples lay sleeping around us on the shore, Jesus silently beckoned me into the lake and, with handfuls of water, washed my ugly spinal wound and said "Your sins are forgiven." My own immediate silent response was characteristic of my managerial impatience—"Forgiveness is the last thing I need."

Since I was so obviously in the hands of a known miracle worker, I wanted my ten-inch tumor out of me and gone (surgery had removed only ten percent of its gray entangled mass after chiseling the backs off numerous vertebrae). So I dared to push past forgiveness and to ask Jesus if I were healed—"Am I also cured?" Plainly it hadn't occurred to me to wonder why the Son of God would have chosen to wash my particular wound in a teeming world of dire sickness. But after a pause that signaled reluctance, Jesus said "That too" and walked away from me as the encounter ended.

These many years later, after an initial prognosis of eighteen months, I'm alive and appear to be strong. So I have no hesitation in believing that—at that moment in midlife burdened with decades of error from small to huge—I needed forgiveness more than I needed healing. For all the years since, though, the fact has remained that I was healed—or that my eventual healing was guaranteed in the wash of that forgiveness—on one clear alternate dawn in Galilee. Yet with all that, I've grown no better at reading my personal failings as a forecast of my fate. I expect I never shall.

It hardly needs stressing that such a blindness is one I share with a large number of contemporary self- and culturally-absolved citizens; but whenever I'm compelled to face clear-eyed the question of the cause of evil in our lives, I'll admit again that direct punishment for personal sin plays only a small role in my deepest instincts in the matter. It would be absurd, however, to doubt that huge quantities of apparent evil are visited by human beings *upon* one another—men, women, and children in whatever degrees of culpability or innocence.

An octogenarian Dominican priest has gone so far as to say to me recently that his own belief on the nature of evil, after a lifetime of mission work, is simple—"It's all people. All evil comes from us." But unless we believe that malevolent humans may exert some form of black magic at a distance, it would seem unquestionable that we must revise my friend's assertion and concede that many forms of extreme suffering—especially crimes against the weak and all assaults on children—arise from initially inexplicable causes such as natural violence, congenital genetic flaws, overwhelming infections, and apparent accidents.

We don't need to recite again at this point one of the refrains of modern Western thinking (that passage in Dostoyevsky's *The Brothers Karamazov* in which an eloquent yet sophomoric Ivan declares that he cannot bow to a god who tortures a single innocent child); but the page is so well known that a simple mention of it may stand for the heart of what I'll call the nadir of mystery. The worst of all events that can befall our selves, our loved ones, or our people are the appalling if not killing stretches of our lives in which God is silent and, in that silence, appears to torment us or someone near to us for no reason discernible by the human mind.

If we're not to believe that all such events come directly from the Creator and his active will, what choices have we? A quick assortment of the classical answers would include the possibilities that

1. The Creator permits all atoms of this universe to pursue their own destinies. If certain atoms form molecules and evolve into, say, the Ebola virus, then that evolution implies at least passive permission from the Creator.

2. God likewise permits or causes certain atoms to form into human beings (such as Hitler) or other creatures (such as rabid hyenas) which are then permitted to work their violent will upon us.

3. Some proto-creature or creatures, like Adam and Eve, chose to offend God and, so, brought the punishment of suffering upon themselves, their descendants, and the whole of nature.

4. God has created a subsidiary power, such as Satan who appears in the Hebrew book of Job and, implicitly, throughout Christian scripture—a power who visits trials upon creation with at least the passive knowledge of God. Jesus acknowledges the power of such a creature but offers no explanation of its origins or its full purpose.

5. The benign Creator is not alone behind the screen of matter and distance. An independent and malign antagonist exists who sometimes tri-

umphs over God's paternal love and freely
wreaks havoc on us and our neighbors.

6. There is no Creator and there never was.
The universe is pure unillumined matter where
senseless atoms and vicious creatures stage the
awful pageants of their wills.

Each of the six guesses presents its own mysteries.
I've already stated my bafflement at any rational and
watchful person's claim of atheism (a creation without
a Creator being even more unimaginable than the
mind and intentions of a single such Maker). And
I've omitted, perhaps unjustifiably, the possibility that
God is, even by human ethical standards, a sadist. For
me, the amount of natural beauty and patent goodness
in the world (whatever the quantity of evil) eliminates
that option and again, in part, the sixth.

The first four options are subject to an objection
of inconsistency. If God permits or encourages atoms
and complex life-forms to work their individual wills
at the expense of the happiness of others, then we
must concede that God's procedures are not invari-
able. His responses, in time if not eternity, to given
human actions like adultery or murder are famously
inconsistent and are never explained, not to the living. Clearly many perpetrators of wrongs and crimes
live long and unpunished lives.

Yet God appears often to lean in unpredictably to alter physical laws and to balk the power of his Satan and then to tilt the board of the universe in a direction which God desires. A plague mysteriously burns itself out, a rampant brain tumor suddenly remits and vanishes, a nuclear standoff on the order of the Cuban missile crisis of 1962 dissolves in a matter of hours.

To the fifth guess—the possible existence of a rival negative power in the universe—I can only say that neither I nor any practicing Christian, Jew, or Muslim known to me has claimed to detect (even in grim ordeals) the presence of such a dark and uncontrolled power. We speak casually or comically of the Devil's making us do so and so; but though I've heard occasional stories of modern exorcisms that give me serious pause, finally there seems to me no necessity for Satan or any other demonic power—not immensely powerful demons, in any case—in the workings of our world.

And nothing of which I'm aware, in my dim awareness of modern cosmology and theoretical physics, predicts the necessity of such a countervailing force. To the contrary, more than a few distinguished physicists believe themselves to be on the near edge of discovering a single unifying equation which will account for all physical phenomena, none of which appear to depend upon the existence of an evil cause.

But is evil somehow inherent in matter? Was it primordially present in creation, some element which God willed to be there or some inherent characteristic of matter which he did not or could not eliminate (Einstein wondered "Did God have a choice?")? In one of the most interesting guesses—in *Paradise Lost*, book seven—Milton appears to adopt and enrich an idea from the *Zohar*, a cabalistic Hebrew tract of the Middle Ages, and to explain the existence of evil by having God announce at the moment of creation that, since he *is* literally everything that exists at that point and since he *fills* the whole of space, he must withdraw a part of his essence from some portion of space so that there may be something which is not himself.

Further, in Milton, God declares that his withdrawal is to take a particular form. He'll retract his *will* from a portion of space and then choose to "put not forth his goodness" into those vacated atoms of himself which he'll employ in constructing the universe and all its creatures. In Milton, as in some Jewish mystical thinking, God is determined to make a thing which is not himself but is free of the ongoing goodness of his will.

We are, then, literally made from atoms of God's own being; but we lack his will and are therefore free to do good or evil as our own natures guide us. The scholar Denis Saurat has even wondered whether, in his retraction from matter, Milton's God may simultaneously have expelled certain destructive tendencies that were present in his own original substance. If God performed some such purge on himself, he appears to have created no receptacle for that destruction other than ourselves and our world.

But orthodox Christian theology has always held—against the *Zohar* and Milton—that God made the universe literally from nothing, *ex nihilo.* And that belief commits its adherents to an even more enormous difficulty in any attempt to explain the existence of evil in the nature of things. Even if we deny that God is whimsically inconsistent, though, or that his power is limited by an opposing power—even by some recalcitrance in the very nature of matter—we're back at your initial puzzlements. Is there a Creator who remains aware of the ongoing details of his creation; and if so, does he care for some or all of those lives?

Recent theologians have spent much ingenuity in arguing that God himself suffers, for us and alongside us, and that our own experience of evil should be mitigated or at least companioned by that fact. They suggest that God suffers not only for, say, the persecution of his chosen people, the Jews, or in his incarnation as the agonized Jesus on the cross; but also, and mysteriously, God suffers from all eternity because he has chosen to love his creation and all lovers suffer. He suffers as well in his encounters with what is called nonbeing.

Insofar as I can comprehend such assertions, they

seem to me insubstantial—more nearly exercises in a near-medieval narrative fantasy than the results of patient commonsensical observation of the world and its creatures. If God is, for instance, omnipotent and omniscient as most creeds contend that he is— if, above all, God created the universe and since he is not human in the range of his emotions—then he well knows that any suffering he may undergo can do him no permanent harm since he is, alpha and omega, the enduring author of the long but ongoing and ultimately benign tale of universal history—the finished tale of his creative will, his justice, and love. No other living and suffering thing has such an advantage. It is suffering that kills us.

So again I'd assert, on the grounds of faith and experience, that a living Creator knows of my life at any moment he chooses to know. In the times of his absence or silence, I've never felt that he was prevented from reaching me, only that he was choosing his distance and for unstated reasons. I'd further claim that he has rescued me since infancy from several life-or-death crises, though occasionally that rescue has come after serious damage was sustained by my body or the body and mind of another creature whom I'd consciously chosen (in fairly normal moments of hunger or malice) to harm. In none of those crises, however, nor in the welcome rescues have I felt the presence of what I'd call a *father*—the strongest imaginable guardian, yes, but far more silent and unpredictable than anything I'd hope to call *abba* in this world, if Aramaic were my informal language.

Indeed, if I assume that you and I are not human monsters—and I have no hint that you're a monster by the standards of Jewish and Christian ethics—then I have to wonder whether those hard-thought traditions have erred radically in insisting so relentlessly on our thinking of God, above all, as our "father." A close look at canonical scripture should give any Jewish or Christian counselor considerable pause at this point. A search through Hebrew scripture, for instance, might well astonish a number of modern rabbis, priests, ministers, and lay people.

In the entire Torah—the first five books of Hebrew scripture—they'll find that God is directly referred to only once as a "father" to his people Israel or to any individual human being. That reference comes as late as Deuteronomy 32:6 in the Song of Moses. A second passage in Deuteronomy 1:31 says that God has "carried his people like a father." References to the fatherhood of God elsewhere in Hebrew scripture are scarce, even in the later prophets and the book of Psalms where we might expect a dense thicket of them.

And even in God's awesome actual appearance to Moses on Sinai in Exodus 34, when the God (who has recently been fuming and sparking terribly in clouds from the height of the mountain) descends into Moses' presence and surprisingly defines himself as "a loving God, kind, slow to anger, full of mercy and truth . . . forgiving wrong and trespass and sin," he continues with an unexplained and apparently contradictory threat, "not entirely leaving guilt unpunished, visiting the wrong of fathers on children, on children of children to the third and fourth generation." That dissonant prophesy from the mouth of God himself—a promise so eternally renewed in the ongoing history of his chosen people and the whole human race—would elicit hectic laughter were its long inky shadow not so daunting as to strike all hearers dumb.

In Christian scripture, it's in the Gospels that we encounter the peculiarly personal, enormously influential, and never-explained insistence by Jesus of Nazareth that God is both his personal father and apparently our own—I'll examine that word *apparently* below. The facts that two of the four Gospels describe Jesus' virgin birth (and that early rabbinical lore seems to assert that Jesus was the illegitimate child of the Jewish girl Miriam and a Roman soldier Panthera) suggest a mystery about Jesus' paternity which may have caused him considerable childhood pain, especially in a village as small as Nazareth.

Recall, for instance, that in Luke 2—the last story

which Luke tells us of Jesus' childhood—the twelve-year-old boy chooses surreptitiously to remain behind when Mary and Jesus' foster father Joseph have left Jerusalem on their Passover visit. After a three-day search, his parents (as Luke calls them) find him in the Temple, talking with the elders. When Mary asks the boy if he didn't realize how anxiously she and his father had searched for him, Jesus ignores her anxiety and her implication that Joseph is his father by saying "Didn't you know I must be in my father's house?" (or "among my father's things"). So unusual is this boy's certainty that, as I was discussing the matter recently with a friend, he wondered if Satan's first temptation to Jesus in the wilderness might not have been the temptation to think of God too literally as his "father."

Whatever the actual history of Jesus' life, it's powerfully stressed in Mark's account of his baptism and in numerous speeches in Matthew and Luke that God is not only Jesus' father and ours but that God is at least as attentive, sympathetic, and available to our prayers and regrets as the best of human fathers might be. Yet whether we adopt or reject the conviction of the early Jesus sect that Jesus, in his crucifixion, bore upon his back the sins of humankind in a final atonement, I'm still left with a keen awareness of one of the great verbal silences in Mark's prime Gospel, a silence as dismaying as any of God's promises is consoling.

How often do Christians (Christian comforters especially) note that in Mark 14:36—for the first reported time and on the last night of his earthly life—Jesus withdraws from his disciples in the garden of Gethsemane, only a few hundred yards downhill from the gleaming Holy Temple; and there alone in the grip of dread, he beseeches God as *abba*, intimate father. He asks *abba* to take away the appalling cup of sacrifice that confronts him so closely and apparently inescapably—an imminent public death by exposure, flogging, and crucifixion.

At the moment of that plea, Jesus is even more entirely alone than he'd been in his early forty days of lonely trial in the Dead Sea desert (in the desert he was after all visited by Satan, wild animals, and angels). Beyond him in the garden, the most trusted of his disciples have fallen asleep, though he'd asked them to keep watch. And just uphill, he must know, the priests and the Romans are assembling their arrest cohort. Even Mark, for all his generally unflinching gaze, cannot bring himself to report (or to imagine) what Jesus says to God at the terrible moment when he acquiesces to *abba*'s remorseless will that Jesus must die tomorrow. Can anyone, from whatever culture in whatever time, expect such distance from a loving father? Some ancient manuscripts of the Gospel of Luke, chapter 22, add a sentence at this dark moment—"An angel from Heaven appeared to him, strengthening him"—but Mark and Matthew preserve the terror of the moment with no mitigation.

As for Jesus' culminating thoughts at the end of his fruitless wait for *abba*'s pity, we only know that when Jesus returns for the final time to wake his sleeping intimates, he tells them to "get up"; and then in Mark's account he uses a Greek verb that is translated many ways—the word *apechei*. The King James and the Revised Standard versions, for instance, translate the verb as "It is enough," an apparently meaningless remark (*what* is enough—the disciples' stolen nap?). But the most recent evidence from excavated contemporary business records indicates that *apechei* was largely used as an indication of payment or receipt in commercial transactions. Jesus has said, in other words, "It's paid" or "Paid" or "It's satisfied"—humankind's vast debt to the Father. In his solitary agony and in the face of *abba*'s silence or fixed refusal, Jesus has acceded to the inevitable and agreed to pay the sacrificial price for the saving of humanity.

So on the next afternoon—nailed to the cross (and again on the witness of Mark, the oldest gospel)—when Jesus addresses God for the final time, he no longer presumes to use the language of filial intimacy. He uses no words of his own at all but only a desperately recalled verse from a Hebrew psalm: "My God, my God, why have you forsaken me?" That's surely as desolate a dying cry as any thoughtful creature ever uttered; and only Matthew has the courage to copy Mark in reporting such final anguish in a man—perhaps a man often reviled as a bastard in his village childhood—who, in the human frailty of youth and hope, had perhaps misread or excessively simplified the nature of God's "fatherhood."

—For that's what I hear your letter asking me first and last: if God created this universe and all its contents and if he continues to exist and intends to be a fatherly God, then what kind of father will permit or fail to intervene in your particular ordeal with cancer—an ordeal that comes so early in a life that you've hoped to dedicate to the healing of others?

The most nearly honest and hopeful guess I can make is that, if you survive this ordeal in working condition, you're almost certain to be a far more valuable medical doctor and person than you'd otherwise have been. Poets more ancient than Aeschylus have hymned the awful paradox that humankind can apparently only advance through suffering; but no one has cut that paradox in deeper letters than Aeschylus—

It is God's law that he who learns must suffer.
And even in our sleep, pain that cannot forget,

falls drop by drop upon the heart, and in our
own despite, against our will, comes wisdom to
us by the awful grace of God.

At the least, down the road, you'll face your own
severely ill patients with a candor and sympathy that
cannot be faked and, in fact, are almost never attempted
by a dismaying number of American physicians.

You know better than I what your chances of survival are, or what they feel like; and one of the
choices you've plainly made now is entirely vital —
the choice to wish to live. Another of the great arresting statements on the matter of suffering and defeat
is found in that one book of the Torah in which God
is called Father. In Deuteronomy 30:19, Moses
speaks to his people as God's direct messenger —

> "I call heaven and earth to witness against you
> this day, that I have set before you life and death,
> blessing and curse; therefore choose life, that
> you and your descendants may live, loving the
> Lord your God, obeying his voice, and cleaving
> to him."

Since Moses doesn't define precisely what he means
by *curse*, I'm free to suggest that he means *the will to
die*, the curse of abandoning prematurely a visible

world of immense beauty and endless need, whatever our own immediate pain.

I'm always shocked to be reminded how many people choose, quite early in their lives, to begin their
deaths—and death is by no means always a mere ces-
sation of heart and brain activity. Anyone who's taught
college, as I have for four decades, well knows that a
number of people choose lifelong mental and spiritual
death in late adolescence, if not sooner—the curse of
surrender to the backwash of time and the all but
irreparable friction of trifling or too demanding human
interactions.

Obviously the powerful hope to live a normal
human span is no guarantee that we'll be given those
years by our doctors, our kin, or finally by God. But
without the hope, and the power to sustain that hope
in the face of all deterrents, life will gutter out fast in
the face of assaults. Augustine speaks, late in his life
as the Vandals battered the gates of his North African
city, of God's supreme gift to us, the "gift of perseverance." Your letter gives strong signs of coming from
someone who means to last for a useful while.

Clearly, if you go under soon, I can't know what the
ultimate outcome of your ordeal will be. I can lean on
the hope that you'll go on to some form of conscious
and immortal life in a less mysterious place, a life in
which you'll comprehend and accomplish what may

be dark and closed to you here and now. Such a sentence would seem lunatic to many of my university and writing colleagues but not, almost surely, to Tolstoy or Mahler or Einstein. And in any case, I'll never confirm that such a hope is fulfilled unless I eventually see you in that luminous next place (or is it shaded?). But if I have any unfamiliar thoughts that are likely to prove at all useful to you, they begin at this point; and they'll amount to guesses, not assertions.

They start by recalling again how seldom the oldest strata of Hebrew scripture call God our *father* or find it appropriate to think of him as a family member, however distant. It may also be worth noting that Hebrew scripture provides no representation of the ideal human father to match the lengthy portrait of an exemplary wife and mother in Proverbs 31. Abraham is perhaps the strongest candidate for admirable paternity, but then he obeys God and threatens so earnestly to kill his son Isaac that Isaac thereafter pales to near invisibility.

For the remainder of his role in Genesis, poor Isaac moves as the near-ghost of a man, a man who on his deathbed cannot tell one of his own sons from the other—we're told that his name for God is "The Fear"—and if Isaac had left us a deathbed testament like his son Jacob's in Genesis 49, we might have had more useful guidance from early on in our Western groping toward a fuller knowledge of the diverse nature of our Maker and Keeper.

In the book of Job 38–41, the most probing of all human documents I've encountered on the matter, God is never once called or thought of as Job's father or anyone else's, though strangely—almost tauntingly—God wonders in Job's presence if "the rain has a father." And when the Creator finally reacts to Job's righteous cry and appears at last in the whirlwind, not only does he make no claim of paternity, he also fails to reveal the faintest trace of any craving for the love and intimacy that God sometimes seems to crave in the prophets and in Christian scripture.

On the contrary, in Job 38–41 the entire tone of God's long magnificent speeches is sardonic and grandly dismissive—

> "Where were you when I laid the foundation of
>   the earth?
> Tell me, if you have understanding,
> Who determined its measurements—surely
>   you know!"

And further, God flatly refuses to take note of Job's horrific losses and sufferings; he never so much as glances at Job's specific request for a bill of particulars against him, though that's the request which seems to have brought God forward to defend himself. For all his expansive detail and haunting imagery, in fact, God's answer to Job may be reduced to sixteen sublimely unsatisfying words—"If you were not my active partner from the start of creation, then stay silent now."

Yet however unnourishing such a reply may sound initially, it seems to me to constitute a beginning to the best lead we're given in the face of ultimate mystery in all of Hebrew and Christian scripture—the most reliable weather vane through fair skies and foul for any troubled human being. Perhaps Job's God means something as drastic as this—*Observe that all of creation is the vehicle upon which you pursue the Creator's will. Attempt any change of pace or direction at your own dire peril. Relish the journey for however long it lasts and wherever it goes.*

For the sheer exuberance of God's sublime account of his own creative delight in his creatures is a very odd but unexpected form of offered solace—*See the splendor of all I have made and savor that, for the time you have.* It's well worth noting that Job himself plainly takes some reward from his overwhelming first encounter with the eloquent voice of the solitary dark core of things. Job has actually seen God; and he knows it—

"I had heard of thee by the hearing of my ear,
but now my eye sees thee."

Job apparently finds God's elaborate brag from the whirlwind oddly comforting in its hints of deeper and deeper layers to the enigma of creation, and at last Job repents of having dared to cloud that enigma with self-absorbed questions when obeisance is the only response that's not literally comic in its irrelevance. In fact, I often feel that the chief reward Job receives for his ordeal must be a final burst of helpless laughter—*What a colossal ass I've been! All creation is one immense interwoven joke to entertain the Maker's hours of endless watch.*

In any case, some form of exhilaration must flow irrepressibly from having one's personal agony so gorgeously dismissed by the Supreme Rhetorician as only one more of his infinite array of effects—and dismissed in two long speeches which amount to a connoisseur's catalogue of delights in his own handiwork. But even a casual reader will note that not a gram of what Job has lost—things and loved ones, time and trust—is actually restored, not as Job had known and loved it, though he is of course lavished with imitation replacements. God, as ever, has played for keeps.

There is only one other passage known to me in our tradition that offers comparably honest and useful direction in the face of disaster. In those few lines, again from the Song of Moses in Deuteronomy

32:38–39, God describes his nature in relation to the false gods with whom Israel cheats him—

> Let them stand and help you.
> Let them be your shelter.
> See now that I,
> I am he.
> No gods with me.
> I kill and I raise,
> I hurt and I heal.
> No flight from my hand.

In the face of such unmitigated forthrightness—a bleakness which demands that we accept God's will as our *good* or go without comfort—I'm compelled as a Christian (though an outlaw) to consider as thoughtfully as I can Jesus' convictions, early in his brief career, of God's meticulous attention and tender love. One of the questions I'd have most wanted to ask Jesus, in his resurrection, was his final feelings in the matter of God's fatherhood.

I suspect that Jesus wouldn't have repudiated his early conviction, but surely it would have grown more intricate and perhaps darker for him after his ghastly death on Calvary and those thirty-odd blank hours in the tomb. Surely he'd have granted a wider spectrum of acts and responses to his notion of *father*, a far wider range of expectations than would have been normal for a human Galilean father of his own lifetime. Whatever rights one grants to God the Father, in any case, he takes what he wants. Right or wrong, the Chorus in Milton's *Samson Agonistes* tells the blind humiliated Samson that God "made our Laws to bind us, not himself."

In the years of my own confrontation with cancer, loss, and chronic pain, I repeat that I experienced fairly steadily the sense of being witnessed and accompanied almost always by what seemed God or a full-fledged messenger of God (at an almost invariably silent distance, though some of those messengers were human beings of extraordinary foresight and practical help). And with that companionship, I was ultimately led back into a new and transformed life and work—the trip took more than three years— but, again, I can't recall the sense that what was watching and helping me onward was anything I'd ever known as *father*.

What felt crucial to my survival then was an unshaken certainty that rescue was possible, even for me. Long acquaintance with the text and tenor of the Gospels convinces me that the God who permits the torture and agonized execution of Jesus on Passover does literally restore life to him on Easter morning. That is, I believe that the resurrection of Jesus is, in however unfathomable a way, a visible palpable reality which holds extreme hope for us all. The Jesus who was unquestionably dead on Friday evening was alive on Sunday morning. However inexplicably transformed, he could be touched and smelt. You could eat a meal with him and hear his voice.

Through long decades I've examined, I think, all the alternate ways to explain the astonishing Gospel narratives of his return from death (the most wonderful yet credible is that in John 21). I've examined, from many angles, the still staggering fact that a literal belief in that return strengthened a small handful of Jesus' previously mediocre and terrified colleagues—and his murderous enemy Saul, who becomes the converted apostle Paul—to transform the life and the future of the huge Roman empire in under three centuries. And with no shade of doubt, I can join Paul in his strongest conviction. God has "cared" on a singular occasion of extraordinary promise for our earthly lives and thereafter.

But that conviction serves as no feather bed beneath me, no opiate; for I'm also aware, with less natural consent, of Paul's almost violent insistence that God's love literally hunts down the souls he has chosen for grace. And I likewise glimpse—this time in the book of Hebrews, an early Christian document—a straight shaft onto the fullest truth that I think we can count on when choosing our steps: the dismaying assertion that "It is a terrible thing to fall into the hands of the living God." We can ask for relief, for healing and respite; we can beg for our loved ones. But the hands we're in, at all times, are neither predictable nor intimately knowable. They may cushion us, even deck us out with unasked-for gifts; but they're never less than burning to the touch; and they acknowledge no guidance, no compass but their own.

You'll have gathered then that, in recent years, I've come more and more to wish that the scriptures of Judaism and Christianity—and a great many more modern clergy and counselors—had forthrightly confronted the silence at the very heart of any God we can worship and that they'd observed it more unflinchingly with us, not dimming our view with rose-colored screens and sweet-voiced chatter that are certain to smash or go cold-dumb at the first touch of heat, not to mention the scalding breath of terror at the sight of pained death.

Apart from the few dark-shadowed passages that I've glanced at here, lately it has seemed more and more to me that I must look to a startling moment in the Hindu *Bhagavad Gita* for the guess that comes nearest to my own conjectures in the wake of my own and my loved ones' catastrophes. I'm by no means a deep student of Hindu thought, and I don't claim to be

a guide to its all but infinite sproutings and sudden aus-
terities. Yet in chapters ten and eleven of the *Gita* when
the human charioteer Arjuna turns to the Lord Krishna,
who is an incarnation of the god Vishnu, and asks to see
Krishna in the full panoply of his divine nature,
Krishna grants with a majestic but generous conde-
scension what Job's God so tauntingly withholds.

On the edge of a battlefield in what is now north-
ern India, Krishna reveals to his human companion
as much of the infinite variety of God's nature—his
multitude of faces and functions—as he wishes that
human to bear. God, in brief, is the total godhead
(Brahman is his Hindu name) of which all other
gods are only partial faces or aspects; and Brahman is
the source of literally all things. In fact, God *is* all
enduring things—both what we humans perceive as
good and evil: birth, growth, flowering, decline,
agony, devastation, death. And in that moment of
revelation, which is famous in America as having
occurred to Robert Oppenheimer at the explosion of
the first atomic bomb, Krishna in his most terrible
divine aspect says—

I am come as Time, the waster of the peoples,
Ready for that hour that ripens to their ruin.

Yet Krishna has, only a few moments earlier, revealed—

Whatever in this world is powerful, beautiful or
glorious, that you may know to have come forth
from a fraction of my power and glory.

Even a fool as hardened as I won't hope to urge a
substantial revision at this late date in our Western
sense of the nature and purposes of God, especially the
God who is both our omnipotent Creator and the
mute witness of so much agony in humankind and
among our fellow creatures. But what if we, the heirs
of a radical Asian-desert monotheism onto which was
later grafted the ambiguous and hazardous notion
of the Creator as a loving Father—what if we could
come to the suffocating and fearsome crises of our lives
in the hope of some patient witness from God yet, at
the same time, a perception of God as vast as the one
which the *Gita* both asserts and dramatizes: an awareness that is surely far more usefully consoling than any
unpropped familial expectations, conditioned as they'd
have to be by our unrealistic modern American expectations of the ideal human father?

What if we'd been allowed, in our worship, to grant
and to build into our most urgent expectations the fact
that a fathering God—like Brahman in all his aspects
but unlike our human fathers—may be all things, creative and destructive, to his creatures and that each of
these things is *good*, whatever our immediate evalua-

tion of it, and good precisely because it is the will of that Father and in some way fulfills the intent of his ongoing care for all that exists?

Further still, what if we were emboldened to grant what seems inescapable: that everything which we call *evil* but which does not derive from other human beings, from other live creatures or physical accidents, must derive from God the Father—that these things are therefore his will and are thus not subject to protest or complaint from us but only to whatever solace or exultance we may take in perceiving that our lives are in God's hands and are the object of his conscious will, however terrible in the short run? Wouldn't we be, not only far braver but more certain still that he notes us with his own mysterious purpose? We'd be, paradoxically, hopeful stoics.

The scriptures of Judaism and Christianity, ambiguous and fragmentary as they are in this matter, only just permit us to form the outlines of a similar concept. Our resistance or refusal, our protests at fate, are less than useless. Prayers for mercy and guidance seem answered on occasion, in a great many lives but by no means all. Wouldn't every life and every faith be stronger then, at its farthest-down roots and in the outermost frailest leaves of its reach, if we heard God entirely and granted—by the moment—that God is what *is* or is *in* all that exists: that he is our only choice, in silent agony or singing joy or on the broad calm plains of those days we hardly pause to notice as blessed?

And since the scriptures of most religions insist so strongly that God has made us for his glory and that glorification is pleasing to him—surprising as that mostly deplored human trait may seem in the mover of tides and galaxies—wouldn't that glory be augmented by a wider spectrum of light and dark in our own dim eyes if we saw and granted and tried to live in the glare of a fuller awareness of his being? Again, Job's God agrees that Yes is the required answer to his question.

To glance at only the immediate present, God is surely the full proprietor or the impassive witness of AIDS and Bosnia, Oklahoma City and Rwanda, the thousands of homeless wretches on the streets of any sizable American city (and every city is a packed mine of riches), the children starved for food and love in our towns, and all the billion other facets of this resplendent appalling planet which we inhabit as pawns or angels unaware or the treasured children of an ultimate inexhaustible Father.

What dictionary, in all the world, can give us a definition of *father* that even begins to hint at the deepest dark in the nature of what is called—most perilously—God the Father? If we work to expand that definition slowly and sensibly to respond to all the visible and implicit aspects of God, then we still must acknowledge how adamantly most creeds insist that love does proceed toward us and all the world we inhabit from that vast God. And our hardest challenge becomes an effort to imagine how such a God, in all his polar traits and actions, can be truly and usefully said to love us. Yet nothing less than that baffling effort is called for in any life that hopes to meet the swells and riptides of actual time.

(And here I wonder briefly if women who are understandably concerned to mitigate the oppressively masculine qualities of God in our creeds might want to consider whether the human female gender is not fortunate to have avoided those painful ambiguities which have flowed, and continue to flow so confusingly, from our thinking of God as father. Do we wish to cloud our fullest sense of *woman* and *mother* by adding those further human qualities to the ineffable—a mother who brings us the whole of history with all its maniacs, wars, and plagues? The poets Gerard Manley Hopkins and W. H. Auden appear to feel the linguistic danger of *Father* when they address God as *Sir* in two memorable verse prayers—a half-droll gesture perhaps but one worth noting for its implications. In the whole matter of God's imputed masculine nature, the Roman Catholic and Orthodox communions have recognized the dilemma and wisely afforded themselves the favor of access to the all-compassionate interceding Virgin, the mother of God's human manifestation, not himself. Would we really want, though, our own maternal counterpart to the Hindu goddess Kali in her destructive aspect, smeared as she is with blood and wreathed with skulls? If not, we need to think long and hard about the requirements of our own God's gender.)

I'll finish soon now, or stop anyhow. However simplistic this long set of guesses, I trust you to see that the questions I've asked have been pressed from me in conditions that were much like the ones you know. I wish I thought there was more honest solace to bring a fellow creature as tried as you are. A few of the old and the patently good are said to greet death with unmixed serenity. But even the strongest faith in the promise of eternal reward cannot be expected to render death free of its frowning chill.

Certainly nothing here is meant to diminish for an instant my sense of the grinding wheel you're presently under, the stark bitterness you taste in the premature dawns of a man awaiting the Yes or No of mercy or ruthless time. Nor have I meant to burden you further with darker thoughts than you're otherwise bearing. To the contrary, if any of these speculations has weight, then they surely tend toward calm at a minimum, a

certain stillness if not consolation — one sensible creature's statement of the faith of our species. Any man or
woman as thoughtful as you, as upright in the blast, is
bound to be under steady watch.

In any case, your whole letter gives off the sound
of a mind as fearless as minds get to be; and in that
bracing air, I've risked a candor that surely will not
come on you as new or more confounding than what
you've already cut your own path through. All I'll
append in closing this is another old claim — that,
beyond a doubt, the Creator is far more mysterious
than we can suspect or than human organs will ever
prove capable of comprehending.

I even suspect that God is more of an enigma than
he's capable of telling us, given the fact that he made
us with such limited instruments of perception.
Which is not to say that, with his tacit approval, our
successors may not invent far more delicate instruments for surveying at least the nearer shores of his
being. Meanwhile my own observations suggest, for
instance, that his wit and humor — his concern as the
supreme storyteller for fair and joyous endings
replete with the sweet air of mercy — are nearly as
characteristic of the road he's laid through history as
any trudge through pain toward death.

And that apparently unquenchable taste by God-
the-Ultimate-Narrator is again affirmed by the blissful

and radiant findings in works by craftsmen as different from one another as the aging Beethoven, Verdi, and Wallace Stevens. Though Beethoven was a Christian-reared deist and Verdi and Stevens were at most agnostic, the Beethoven *Missa Solemnis*, the "Libera me" prayer at the end of Verdi's *Requiem*, and the last poems of Stevens exhale an extraordinarily cloudless confidence in the face of decay and death.

For what it's worth, my own conviction, from here in my midsixties, is that a created universe which has evolved the staggering richness of life that we observe on this one planet can scarcely permit that phenomenon to die in eventual cold silence like a candle forgotten in a room deserted by all other life—not unless the components of that flame and its fuel will transform into ongoing and enduring forms of being and consciousness.

Even the law of entropy can't deny that the energy which is steadily dispersed into space may have a destiny grander, or more interesting, than darkness and frigid silence—and I claim that just as the news is announced that the visible galaxies are apparently flinging outward, and apart from one another, toward the perhaps nonexistent walls of the universe at a far faster rate than we'd known. If I and the major part of the human race are wrong in that hope for a conscious endurance, then the worst that faces us is

surely oblivion—purest black rest like that afforded
by the best anesthesia, with which you're likely familiar. No dreams, no fears, no expectations, no waking,
no sense whatever of self or another.

It may be entirely a matter of the outlook I've been
programmed to take ever since the conjunction of
my sanguine and welcoming parents. It may flow from
some lucky gift in my earliest days among often
afflicted but finally laughing kin; but if forced to spec-
ulate, I'd have to say that the mind in the ultimate pith
of things is benign, that it tells itself our long slow
story from a comprehensible taste for *stories*; and only
a mad mind hopes that stories end in crushed lives and
strangled cries. My bred-in-the-bone conviction about
you is that you're bound toward a goodness you can't
avoid and that the amount of calendar time which lies
between you and that destination is literally meaningless to God, though surely of the greatest importance to you.

Apt comfortless sayings, as you must know, are often
brought out when a short life is threatened—*The good
die young* or *Whom God loves, he soon reclaims.* A
quick look at history will, at a minimum, confirm that
God sets little if any importance on the length of a
human life. Think only of Flannery O'Connor dying
at thirty-nine, Raphael and van Gogh at thirty-seven,
Mozart at thirty-five, Simone Weil at thirty-four, Schu-

bert at thirty-one, Emily Brontë at thirty, and Keats at twenty-five.

Yet what human being, facing his own death or that of a loved one, was ever awarded the smallest share of that unplumbed equanimity with which God monitors time from eternity? In my own threatened days, I sometimes glimpsed the chance of calm surrender but never the smiling peace that turns its back on a count of the moments and years doled out to this one or that—the cut-down child, the doddering tyrant. And my hunger for more, and still more, competent working time is unabated.

Whatever you get from God or your own mind or these few pages, be assured at the end here that—once again—all I've said derives from no more than the faith and expectation of a single creature and the lucky disclosures he thinks he's glimpsed in a life already longer than either of his own parents had. If you think I'm mumbling in soft-brained error, I might not deny you. I may be gravely misled in any new notion I've offered.

I know I believe that God loves his creation, whatever his kind of *love* means for you and me. Again, some version of that belief lies near the center of all major creeds. From the range of emotions that might inspire you or me, or another rational human, to create a universe, love seems the one most likely to cause such a mammoth and long-lasting enterprise. The only other imaginable inspiration would seem to be a ravenous brutality or a cold curiosity of unthinkable proportions; and however burdened we and our world may be with intermittent darkness and worse, I suspect that very few human creatures would confess to believing that we're made and managed by a psychopath of universal proportions.

So surely God works and watches, in some sense—no doubt many senses—from love or from some barely imaginable intensification of the ideal lover's feeling for the beloved—an emotion which Augustine defines in the words *Volo ut sis,* "I will you to be" or "I want you to be who you are." I don't claim certainty for much else I've said. But that claim feels like firm ground to me. And it would take more strength than I've got to deny Eliot's still assertion at the end of the *Four Quartets* that

> . . . all shall be well and
> All manner of thing shall be well
> When the tongues of flame are in-folded
> Into the crowned knot of fire
> And the fire and the rose are one. . . .

or Bach's findings at that final moment in the B Minor Mass when somber but glorious horns begin to bloom and then flood the abyss beneath the choir's "Give us peace" or Dante's hard-earned vision at the end of his *Comedy* that the "scattered leaves of all the universe" are gathered inward and bound together in one volume by love, that love which is both the binding and the fuel of all life and all movement—"The love that moves the sun and the other stars." In any case, I'd want you to know that I haven't dealt idly with the questions you ask nor do I, again, share easily the news of your trial.

Now that you've made this first contact, sad news from you would be a harsh discouragement. News of your intact perseverance would be most welcome. If my answer to what you so baldly ask amounts to no more than a stumbling guess, then know that this one long surmise comes from as deep in my mind and nature as I know how to go. Whatever a far-off fellow creature can offer by way of the earnest company of prayer and thought, I offer gladly.

All hope from

REYNOLDS

FURTHER READING,
LISTENING, AND LOOKING

Anyone who's curious to think further into the questions examined in this letter will find mountains of relevant evidence at hand — well beyond the books, music, and art already mentioned. Beyond the widely available summaries of the religious and metaphysical issues, I'll suggest a few other documents that I've found of enduring interest. And since I'm often at least as impressed by the intuitions of artists — poets, novelists, playwrights, painters, composers — as by the mathematically arrived-at deductions of scientists, I've suggested an awareness of the questions and assertions of some of the most far-reaching artists, old and new.

The anonymous book of Job is primary. Try reading it in various translations. Even if you know ancient Hebrew (and Job is apparently the most obscure of canonical Hebrew texts), you're likely to discover numerous rewarding angles. Of modern scholarly editions, I've found help in Marvin Pope's translation and commentary for the Anchor Bible series; and the new translation by Raymond P. Scheindlin is both unusually scrupulous in its faith to the original and full of fresh insights. Stephen Mitchell's version omits a number of lines from the Hebrew text and is often extremely free in its English equivalents, but it has passages of striking comprehension and eloquence, and Mitchell's preface is strong.

Reflections on the sufferings of Job and his eventual acceptance of God's inscrutable will are almost as plentiful as translations. William Blake's set of engravings of the whole Job story are as vivid and memory-enhancing as any verbal commentary. In fact, I know of no other works of graphic art which capture the enigma of suffering more precisely or confront the unapologetic splendor of God more convincingly, but Carl Jung's essay *Answer to Job* and Robert Frost's brief wry verse play *A Masque of Reason* are also useful.

*　　*　　*

The Hebrew and Christian canonical scriptures—the Old and New Testaments of what's called the Bible—are the broad footing to all Western thought on the subjects. The King James Version, universally admired for its beauty and unusual fidelity to the word order and literal diction of the original, is rightly much loved; but its English is now nearly four hundred years old and often confronts a modern reader with obscurities and puzzles. In the biblical passages cited in the letter, I've sometimes employed the reliably close Revised Standard translation, sometimes the freer and less dependable New Revised Standard, occasionally the King James; and in one instance (Deuteronomy 32:38–39), I've resorted to an attempt of my own.

Lacking a knowledge of Hebrew, I made my translation with the aid of numerous literal versions by others. The full version, and many more, are available in my book *A Palpable God* where they are prefaced by an essay which examines the strategies of narrative in general and biblical narratives in particular. They are, after all, far the most successful of human narratives if the compulsion of belief in the tale told is our standard of success.

In my own reading of the Bible, again I most

frequently consult the Revised Standard for its
trim literalness and its reluctance to paraphrase
willfully and inexcusably—a virtue quite scarce
in contemporary translations. A more recent con-
servative translation, admirable in its scrupu-
lousness, is the New International Version. The
New Revised Standard has unfortunately moved
closer toward the practice of speculative paraphrase and the substitution of genderless nouns
and pronouns for the Hebrew and Greek male
originals. Often such substitutes do no significant
violence to the original. On occasion, however,
they are seriously misleading and provide an
atmosphere which, far from honoring the role of
women in sacred events, in fact endangers our
understanding of their unique and generally
benign presence.

Though it may initially seem impenetrably
exotic, or redolent of airport encounters with
importunate flower-selling youth in the 1970s, a
patient reading of the Sanskrit *Bhagavad Gita*
is likely to demonstrate why its central value for
millennia, and for many millions of Hindus,
is enormous and ongoing. The passages I've
quoted from the *Gita* come from the fluent
English version by Swami Prabhavananda and

his student, the novelist Christopher Isherwood. A more recent close translation is by W. J. Johnson. The videotape of Peter Brook's adaptation of the Indian epic, the *Mahabarata*, of which the *Gita* is a part, is greatly condensed but is memorable.

The lines from Aeschylus's tragedy *Agamemnon* are adapted by me from a translation by Edith Hamilton. They were recalled to the press, impromptu from memory and in this same translation, by Robert Kennedy on the night of the murder of Martin Luther King (two more months and Robert Kennedy himself would be murdered). A fluent modern translation of the entire *Oresteia*, the trilogy of plays of which *Agamemnon* is the first part, is by Robert Fagles.

Fagles's translations of Homer's *Iliad* and *Odyssey* provide a vigorous entry into a world so different from our own as to seem both horrendously and enviably extraplanetary, a world in which the hands of the gods are not only frequently detectable in human affairs but are often literally visible and malicious. Homer's is a world in which evil is often lamented but whose presence is never questioned.

*   *   *

The oldest document concerned with the acts and teaching of Jesus of Nazareth is the Gospel according to Mark; and Jesus is, for better or worse, our culture's central suffering figure. Mark appears to have been written between AD 65 and 70; and the oldest witness to its composition claims that it was written by John Mark who was the interpreter of Jesus' chief disciple, Simon Peter.

A number of scholars now doubt that tradition (I don't); but in any case the brief, abrupt, and wildly original document appeared some thirty to forty years after Jesus' death; and my own very close translation of its bare-boned astonishing narrative can be found in *Three Gospels*, a volume which likewise contains a close translation of the Gospel of John and an apocryphal gospel of my own, all three with full introductions.

John is the sole Gospel which claims, within its own text, to derive from the memory of an eyewitness to Jesus' life, death, and resurrection. There are numerous moments in its narrative when eyewitness seems the only explanation for the power of the events described and the speeches given.

The only other explanation would be that a Jewish genius who combined the skills of Shakespeare and Tolstoy appeared in the first-century Middle East, virtually invented the techniques of modern fiction and drama, then vanished with no further trace beyond the three short letters which the New Testament likewise attributes to John. Whoever the author of the Gospel — and the oldest tradition attributes it to Jesus' disciple John son of Zebedee — it appeared some fifty to sixty years after Jesus' death.

A reader who's understandably adrift in the newly revived controversy over the historical reality and the actual teaching of Jesus of Nazareth may welcome the balanced sanity of E. P. Sanders's *The Historical Figure of Jesus*, Raymond Brown's *The Death of the Messiah,* and the multivolume study *A Marginal Jew* by John P. Meier. More radical contemporary views — so notably associated with the Jesus Seminar — are on ample display in the lively, immensely self-assured, sometimes piercing, and often baldly unsubstantiated books and television appearances of John Dominic Crossan. A fair introduction to Crossan's method, and that of his school, is his *Jesus: A Revolutionary Biography.* Like all Crossan's work, it's a frustrating combination of occasional fresh insight and sweepingly destructive guesswork. His *Who Killed Jesus?* is breathtakingly high-handed in its treatment of older, and much more responsible, studies.

An unequaled vision of the heart of a benign universe is found in the final canto of Dante's *Divine Comedy.* Anyone who's skittish about attempting its surprisingly simple fourteenth-century Italian will find numerous adequate translations. I most often use the Carlyle/Oelsner version with the original Italian on facing pages. The nineteenth-century version by Henry Wadsworth Longfellow is close, arresting, and still lucid. Among more recent attempts, John Ciardi's is fresh and clear.

John Milton's poem *Paradise Lost,* in its long account of the fall of Satan from Heaven and his ensuing seduction of the prime man and woman in Eden (our "first parents," as Milton calls them), is a considerably more modern—and, I think, endlessly resourceful—dialogue between an incomparable human mind and every major dilemma a man or woman can face today. And while its ten thousand lines of baroque seventeenth-century English verse may look forbid-

ding, a little persistence in reading (especially
reading aloud) will pay usable dividends. Milton's half-clandestine but plainly probing and
heretical view of God and God's role in evil and
human suffering sets him with the greatest of
prophets and poets from any time or place.

I've mentioned Dostoyevsky's dealings with evil
in *The Brothers Karamazov*. His lesser-known
novel *The Idiot* is involved with similar mysteries.
In general, it's been the nature of the European
and American novel to concern itself with less
dire and less abstract themes, though Melville's
Moby-Dick is an imposing exception; and
Georges Bernanos's *The Diary of a Country Priest*
(one of the very few successful novels about a
genuinely good human being) is rich with suggestions about the contest of evil and goodness.

My own childhood memoir *Clear Pictures*
and my cancer memoir *A Whole New Life* deal
with further aspects of the questions as they've
confronted me, my kin, and friends. My trilogy
A Great Circle (consisting of the novels *The Surface of Earth*, *The Source of Light*, and *The
Promise of Rest*) attempts to follow the work of
providence in the lives of two large intermarried
families and all their surrounding dependents

and places through more than a century of American time.

To my knowledge, though it's nearly a century old, the richest and most provocative study of human experiences with the ineffable is William James's *The Varieties of Religious Experience: A Study in Human Nature.*

Written as a series of lectures for the University of Edinburgh in 1901–2, the chapters proceed nonetheless in a wandering, amiable, even whimsical, voice to examine virtually all aspects—from the repugnant through the laughable to the sublime—of our relations to God or the gods; and they at last come to rest in some guesses of James's own which are hardly likely to convince many readers (his own tendency is toward polytheism).

Yet his gaze at mystical experience and at our relations with good and evil is so relentless as to explode, in a courteously muffled and often good-natured way, any number of spiritual and rational delusions—including the claims of modern science to offer a reasoned floodlit explanation for all those phenomena that much of our race has thought of as transcendent since the earliest records of human thought and feeling.

*   *   *

A more recent and broader-gauged look at the common principles of belief is available in Aldous Huxley's *The Perennial Philosophy*. Any reader who's wary of the Huxley who almost single-handedly midwifed the mescaline and LSD revolution of the 1960s should gain the acquaintance of a mind as level and capacious as the one revealed in this book's gathering of quotes from the prime mystics of East and West and in the lucid commentary which binds the quotations.

T. S. Eliot's *Four Quartets* and Flannery O'Connor's short story "Revelation," written not long before her early death, are as undeceived, illuminating, and convincing as their older companions in verse and fiction. Eliot's sound recording of his poems brings an astonishing clarity to lines that, on the page, may seem impenetrably opaque. O'Connor appears to have left no recordings, but many of her irreverent yet deeply religious letters are collected in the Library of America volume dedicated to her work. No recent artist, in any form, has worked in the oncoming face of premature death with more strength and grace.

*   *   *

Since I've referred unsympathetically to current theological speculation on the notion of a suffering God, in fairness I'll suggest a considerably more favorable summary of modern thought on the subject—*The Creative Suffering of God* by Paul S. Fiddes. I don't contest the claim that the thought of a God who suffers beside us is, at first sight, a consoling prospect; but again I fail to see how God's omnipotent suffering could be at all comparable to our own ultimately powerless struggles.

A recent sane summary of thought on the subject of evil is *Evil: A Historical and Theological Perspective* by Hans Schwarz. It ranges evenhandedly and responsibly from East to West, through the major religious creeds and through modern theological and psychological speculation; but its conclusion is unnervingly optimistic in its view from what might well be called the blindered wing of Christianity—"Although we will not always be victorious, we need not fear that evil will devour us. God himself has set boundaries for evil that it cannot overstep." Such an anodyne claim comes from a German theologian born in 1939. Though his book ends there, Schwarz would likely point out that, however ferociously

Hitler devastated his world, the devastation ended after twelve years—not soon enough for the many millions killed.

A broad and generally reliable survey of the major ongoing human faiths is Huston Smith's *The World's Religions.* The son of parents who were Christian missionaries in China, Smith maintains nonetheless a broad sympathy with histories and traditions quite different from his own; and his control of both the minutiae of various beliefs and their broader implications is impressive.

There are more than a few books by scientists or knowledgeable writers which attempt to detect in contemporary physics, cosmology, and mathematics the possibilities, or lack thereof, of belief in an intervening creator. Most of them, however elementary, have proved too technical for me (as Stephen Hawking's famous *A Brief History of Time* has likewise proved impenetrable, not only for me but for virtually everyone I know who has attempted to read it). One book that just barely remains comprehensible for me, and that appears to be scientifically competent, is *The Fire in the Equations: Science, Religion and the*

Search for God by Kitty Ferguson. Ferguson provides, as well, a lengthy bibliography of other relevant and sometimes contradictory views. In *The Faith of a Physicist*, John Polkinghorne, who is both a physicist and an Anglican priest, provides a comprehensibly argued examination—and a final affirmation—of the essential articles of the orthodox Christian creed in the light of the principles of contemporary physics. His *Belief in God in an Age of Science* requires more sophistication from the reader than I, at least, can summon.

To turn to Western music (my knowledge elsewhere is sadly limited), an interested listener can find almost infinite resources. Beginning with the lately popular Gregorian chants and the eerily visionary hymns of the medieval Abbess Hildegard of Bingen, a patient listener may find much challenge and eventual knowledge in the voluminous masses, cantatas, oratorios, and other rites of Palestrina, Monteverdi, Cavalli, Tallis, Purcell, Bach, Handel, Haydn, Mozart, Beethoven, Schubert, Verdi, Bruckner, Brahms, and hundreds of worthy others. More recent composers with recurrent transcendental concerns include Mahler, Elgar, Rachmaninoff, Stravinsky, Poulenc, Barber, Messiaen, and Pärt.

Almost all those verbal works are in print, in some form, and can be supplied by an ample library or a serious bookstore. However brief a list from a world of worthy studies, any of those texts — long or short, in English, Hebrew, Greek, Sanskrit, Russian, or French — might prove to be the start for a lifetime's reading in matters as baffling yet as beckoning as any.

Performances of the music described may be found — frequently in abundance and with other relevant works by an enormous list of composers — in a good CD store or mail-order service. Anyone willing to forge into the ancient and still continuing reserves of Hebrew, Hindu, Buddhist, Islamic, and other Asian and African sacred music will likewise find many examples. The chants of Tibetan Buddhist monks, Indian ragas, and the drummed rhythms by which Islamic Sufis enact their whirling ecstatic dances are soon, if not instantly, recognizable to Western ears as hymns of supplication, adoration, fear, praise, and devotion to the unseen Creator.

The store of images — drawn, painted, chiseled, molded — which celebrate that same force is even more abundant. They range from the brilliant paintings in the recently discovered Chauvet cave in France (which are, at more than thirty thousand years old, the first known human paintings) through the teeming millennia of sacred art from virtually every recorded civilization on all inhabited continents. It's a big claim but I think it's accurate to say that no culture has agreed to value or preserve for long any substantial quantity of art which has seemed to deny the existence of transcendental reality.

Any sizable library can show thousands of reproductions of sacred art starting with the Chauvet cave, the caves at Lascaux and Altamira, and in temples, cathedrals, churches, mosques, and galleries descending to the present. That art constitutes a large portion—if not the totality—of the creative legacy of many ancient, medieval, and more recent civilizations in Africa, Asia, Australia, Europe, and the Americas down to today's intricate and sand-painted mandala, carefully made by Buddhist monks to honor the unseen, then scattered to the winds.

Though they have not been an insistent theme of fashionable art in the West since early in the nineteenth century, transcendental themes—even hints of yearning—are detectable in a good deal of abstract expressionist painting, most famously in the late work of Mark Rothko. And the landscapes in painters like Edward Hopper and Odd Nerdrum have, almost unavoidably, kept alive a tradition as old as Chinese scroll paintings of rivers and mountains or medieval European paintings of cities and farms. It's a rare landscape from any century—or seascape, cloudscape—that doesn't suggest to many of its viewers an immanent or hovering intelligent presence beyond the painter's hand and eye. More than a century of photographs and motion pictures have made their own contributions to the whole.

Finally, to explain what may seem an omission, I'll glance at the enormous body of literature that concerns itself with the investigation of evil. Interesting, if profoundly obscure, documents like the Egyptian and the Tibetan Books of the Dead are available in modern translations. Not specifically devoted to the study of evil but to the escape from evil, those two documents are largely concerned with practical counsel on surviving the dangers of death; and as such they stand on the side of life.

Available—if less easily found—are huge multinational assortments of magical spells, ceremonies of exorcism, and incantations for summoning the aid of demons or of the embodiment of evil himself. Serious, if often bizarre, medieval and modern Hebrew cabalistic speculations and similar Christian exotica stand at the head of a continuing body of transfixed contemplation of evil that ranges from the all but uncrossable deserts of nineteenth-century Theosophy to the latest American Satanist tracts. Most such tracts that I've seen are self-denying in their intellectual confusion and vapidity, though alas (in every age and place) there seem to be readers prepared to take them as goads to actual malice and violent action.

Since I share the common experience that evil will find each human life, with no need of summoning, I have studiously avoided any extensive familiarity with such work and can therefore offer no guide to its accumulated layers. Yet the possibility—if not the likelihood—that evil indeed exists, as a primeval and continuing power beyond us, continues to leave me respectful of its possible presence or imminent arrival.

Anyone who doubts that possibility should read Daniel Goldhagen's *Hitler's Willing Executioners: Ordinary Germans and the Holocaust,* a recent historical study that—despite widespread controversy in the United States and Europe about its methods of inquiry—provides near-overwhelming evidence for the existence of an immense core of mystery in the nature of evil: a famished power that may seize any human, or virtually an entire people, and employ them like dolls of a vicious and all but unstoppable fury. And the fact that the phenomenon of triumphant Nazism began the year I was born and ran its full murderous course by the time I was twelve years old is a homely reminder for me and many others of my still vital generation of an eternal threat.

Once entered upon, of course, a taste for the history of modern human or demon-possessed human evil may be fed in numerous wide-ranging accounts. To begin with our own history, there are unanswerable studies of the extermination of American Indian populations, of the American slave trade, and three hundred years of slave life. A balanced but withering account of the Indian wars and massacres is *The Invasion of America: Indians, Colonialism, and the Cant of Conquest* by Francis Jennings. A powerful succinct history of slavery is Peter Kolchin's *American Slavery: 1619–1877*; and Eugene Genovese's *Roll, Jordan, Roll: The World the Slaves Made* evokes the stubborn and protean richness of slave life in the face of unyielding blindness and malice.

Other cultures can offer histories of those twentieth-century devastations perpetrated in the name of Leninist-Stalinist and Maoist Marxism and Pol Pot's Khmer Rouge. Whatever up-to-date slaughters and afflictions our fiendishly inventive race has awarded itself will be the subject of CNN's ever-grim report every moment of the clock. History pants to run abreast of the brisk unflagging pace of evil, whatever its motive force and fuel; yet the proportional number of Homo sapiens who doubt the existence of a conscious Creator—the source of all good if nothing more—is likely no greater than it's ever been.

REYNOLDS PRICE

Reynolds Price was born in Macon, North Carolina in 1933. Educated in the public schools of his native state, he earned an A.B. *summa cum laude* from Duke University; and in 1955 he traveled as a Rhodes Scholar to Merton College, Oxford University to study English literature. After three years and the B.Litt. degree, he returned to Duke where he continues in his fifth decade of teaching. He is James B. Duke Professor of English.

In 1962 his novel *A Long and Happy Life* received the William Faulkner Award for a notable first novel and has never been out of print. Since, he has published more than thirty books. Among them, his novel *Kate Vaiden* received the National Book Critics Circle Award in 1986. His *Collected Stories* appeared in 1993, his *Collected Poems* in 1997; in 1995 he completed his trilogy *A Great Circle*, which consists of the novels *The Surface of Earth*, *The Source of Light*, and *The Promise of Rest*. He has also published volumes of plays, essays, and two volumes of memoir *Clear Pictures* and *A Whole New Life*. The latter is his account of a long survival of spinal cancer and ensuing paraplegia. He is a member of the American Academy of Arts and Letters, and his books have appeared in sixteen languages.